OXFORD POETS 2002

The editors of this anthology are members of the OxfordPoets Board.

David Constantine is an authority on Hölderlin, as well as a poet and translator. His most recent collection is *Something for the Ghosts* (Bloodaxe, 2002).

Hermione Lee, Goldsmiths' Professor of English Literature at Oxford and Fellow of New College, is author of *Virginia Woolf* (1996) and other biographical and critical works.

Bernard O'Donoghue teaches Medieval English at Wadham College, Oxford and has published four books of poems of which the most recent is *Here Nor There* (Chatto, 1999).

Also available from Carcanet/Oxford*Poets*:

Oxford Poets 2000
Oxford Poets 2001

Oxford*Poets* 2002

an anthology edited by
David Constantine, Hermione Lee
and Bernard O'Donoghue

OxfordPoets

CARCANET

First published in Great Britain
in 2002 by
Carcanet Press Limited
4th Floor, Conavon Court
12-16 Blackfriars Street
Manchester M3 5BQ

A CIP catalogue record for this book
is available from the British Library

ISBN 1 903039 62 2

The publisher acknowledges financial
assistance from the Arts Council of England

Set in 10pt Palatino by Bryan Williamson, Frome
Printed and bound in England by SRP Ltd, Exeter

Contents

Introduction   ix

Anne Berkeley
24 February   3
The Men from Praga   3
Gasometer   4
Matthew Crampton   5
They   6
Brian in the All-Night Cafe   7
River   8
After Séeberger   9
Pauahi Crater 10 am   10

Roy Blackman
Even though we don't wear Walkmans   13
Not long now   14
Turning the kitchen setts   15
Creating   15
The Watermen   16

Sasha Dugdale
On Kolomenskoe Embankment   19
For Akhmatova   19
'There is light streaming from an upstairs window'   20
'Under a shower'   20
Yalta   21
Madonna in the Meadow   22
Letters   23
'I breathed in at night'   24
'The wide glass sky'   25
'In a Chinese city'   25
Assuming human form   26
Corps de Ballet   27
Chalk and Cheese   28

Stuart Henson
The Train to Nowhere   31
The Cannonball   31
Under the Shadows   32
from *Mountain Time*
   Up There   33
   Cemetery of the Four Knolls   33

Martha Kapos
The Night Kitchen   39
An Angel Entered the Picture   40
Yes and No   41
Mute   42
Equator   43
Cosmology   43
A Child is the Sea   44
The Narrow Kiss   46
Pantomime   47
Tree-Poem for Apollo   49
The Origin of the Sexes According to Aristophanes   50
The Blackberry   50

Hugh McMillan
Wandered   55
My Mother's Dictionary   55
A Curse on Sister Owens   56
Old Photograph   57
Wildlife   58
Marked   59
A Very Short History of the Darien Scheme   61
Room 3   61
On the Coast of North West England   62
The Curse of Atreus   63
Remember   63

Richard Meier
Dreamlike   67
Phil   67
Ablutions   68
Adults   69
Solo   69
In Case of Fire   70
Tracing Paper   70
Relative   71

Introduction

This is the third OxfordPoets Anthology – already the beginnings of a tradition. Our programme remains, quite simply, to publish good new poetry; and in doing that we give house room (scarcer and scarcer nowadays) to some poets who already have a deserved reputation and to others who, so we believe, soon will have.

The first two Anthologies sold well; and were successful also in that several of the writers introduced in them have since appeared with full collections to their names. The series has already made a significant contribution to contemporary English verse. The present volume is equally promising. It has great variety of tone, technique, locality and subject. Of itself, in a small compass, it is living proof of poetry's ability to deal with any aspect of the lives we live now.

ANNE BERKELEY

Anne Berkeley lives near Cambridge. She is a member of the performance group Joy of Six. Her pamphlet *The buoyancy aid and other poems* was published by Flarestack in 1997.

Of the poems in this anthology, '24 February' won first prize in the Kent & Sussex Poetry Competition 1998, 'The Men from Praga' won 1st prize in the Blackwells/*TLS* Poetry Competition 2000, 'Gasometer' won a prize in the *Tabla* Poetry Competition 2000, 'Brian in the All-Night Café' and 'River' were first published in *Smiths Knoll* and 'After Jean Séeberger' was first published in *The Interpreter's House*.

24 February

To get some air, if there were any air,
Mr McLurcan brought the parrot up on deck.
Its cage, wrought & gilded like the Koh-i-Noor's
at the Crystal Palace, wobbled & squawked. The parrot
swung by its beak from the bars: I saw it peer out
through one crazy eye, desperate
for leaves, jackfruit, a tender from port.
When he opened the door it seemed to pour out,
up in a flash, in the arc of a maroon
to the rigging, where it blustered from spar to
spar like St Elmo's fire. Everyone stared & shouted.
There was all the sea, level as a field of wheat,
between here and Ascension for it to get lost in
but it sneered & chewed a claw with its pewter tongue
& then hunted through all the bare forest of our ship
for leaves, nuts, berries, another parrot
or any trace of any green thing.
There was only the mustard & cress I had sown
sprouting down in the dark of our cabin.
Mr McLurcan turned back to his carving.
He'll be down soon enough, when he's hungry.
Wind in night. Forty days out of Melbourne.
Black Albatross raffled for the Seamen's Mission.

The Men from Praga

Because my Polish doesn't run to 'tram ticket',
I have to walk. And my camera's jammed.
I jab it with my gloves. Brush at orange grit
the wind flings off the tarmac. It's miles.
And anyway, the light's gone.

Over the bridge, across the Vistula, is Praga –
the Bear-Pit, the badlands, the concrete tower blocks.
The sky weighs down on the river, beats it flat,
squeezing out the scum that snags on reeds.
I imagine heavy industries upstream.

But it isn't scum. Ice. Its visible edge. Because,
down on the river, far from shore:
two men crouch on camp-stools, hauling
something in from the tricky gleam, doing
delicate, intricate things with their bare hands.

I watch them. They're quite at home
out there in the channel. Smoking, fixing bait.
The wind flicks Polish at me. It's all beyond me –
their Sunday morning ease, their ice,
the fluent fish at large below their feet.

Gasometer

I used to run past Gas Street, afraid
the merest whim would spark it off. It loomed green
over everything, the garlic smell warning
of strange powers. It went up and down
like moods, the whole town lit up and cooking.

The North Sea bubble blew it out.
Around the country, empty gantries lingered
beyond notice on the skyline, rusting and redundant,
to be wrenched apart by economic forces,
oxy-torches and an engine with a shear.

Which is why I'm up here, nose-down on this dome
where they're peeling back the skin: rivet-dimpled,
with blooms of colour where the torch has cut.
Paint flakes and catches underneath my nails.
Unconcealed, the tank goes deeper than I'd thought.

The edge I'm leaning on creaks slightly
but it's warm in the sun as my camera gropes
for the secrets of its structure, how in the dark
it swelled with power on a raft of water and floated up
to the very top. This broken, empty thing – I want

it whole again, the spokes and posts re-covered
as the welders left them, sealed under me and rising . . .
Guide-wheels squeak up pillars and in the yard
they're shovelling coke, and gas is filling darkness
half an inch below me, lifting me into the view.

Matthew Crampton

Matthew Crampton lived for a glimpse of heaven –
twenty years in poverty on a hilltop,
every morning praying for light or weather,
washed in the dewpond.

He prepared his soul as he fed the chickens,
hoed the stones, recorded his every scraping;
every evening prayed and untied his sandals,
wrote in his diary.

Came the year when snow never left the mountains.
Seedcorn finished. Cannibal bantams, he wrote,
nothing for it now but to show them mercy,
twisted their heads round.

Firewood all gone, furniture, feathers – Matthew
burned his diary, lay on the mattress-shadow
on his left side, facing the only window,
watching the sunset.

They

Sleep's a fragile thing – a sound is dying –
bark like muntjac gone before you've heard it,
reminding you of something, like a conscience.

The vixen and owl ignore our roads,
our ways of thinking. They have their own
maps and reasons for their screams.

Out there with them in the damp
up to no good, down the other path,
with eyesight keen enough to need no moon,

mostly silent, moist-tongued and always hungry,
sniffing at the hazelbush, running perhaps,
careful not to let the dry stick crack

or the latch click on the hencoop or the car
door slam twice, the stray thoughts,
disowned for crimes of being

right or wrong or inconsolable,
hunt and couple and redouble.
You must know something of this,

staring through wiped windows in the dark
into another train that isn't there, another set of eyes
focusing through yours into the rain. You'd think

they'd come running on a wet November evening,
when streetlamps gather haloes of wet twigs,
they'd edge round light from study windows, watching.

They never answer when I call them
through the emptied spaces.
I've never seen them but I know they're there.

Call them our 'drathers and our failures,
our esprits de l'escalier, it's not they who have escaped.
Their day will come. They know how they outnumber us.

Brian in the All-Night Café

He's on his second cup, and does it again:
tears carefully apart with both hands,
little finger flicking the shooshing cascade.
He stares as if his whole life centred
on this ritual of sugaring,
stirs it into circles that draw him down and down.

While he's drinking his coffee he will think
of his wife's habit of clearing her throat before speaking,
that little *huh-huh* he wants to stop,
but it's been too long now – he's hardly aware
of when it started, it was suddenly always there
announcing the least mention of dinner, of rain.

He has another packet of sugar, turning and tapping it,
forefinger and thumb turning and tapping.

And it's been so long he can hardly
mention it now, and even if he did,
she wouldn't be able to stop, so
why make two of them unhappy?

Turning and tapping the unopened
sachet of brown sugar on the yellow formica.

But perhaps he should say something now
so she knows to step out of his way
one day when it will become
unbearable, as it nearly has. And he reaches
for the slopped cup's thick white handle.

River

His deep voice gets you up in the morning,
always in a hurry, no time for nonsense.

In his grubby string vest he muscles down the valley,
singing loudly, sweeping away all objections.
At night you hear his murmur, grown-up through floorboards.

His temper is huge but predictable.
He always knows where he's going. When thwarted,
knows no bounds. Then you need
oilskins, gumboots, a quick boat out of town.

Sometimes he'll bring you a surprise: fish,
a little canoe, a dragonfly. He keeps
a kingfisher up his sleeve for nostalgia.
Sometimes there'll be algae for days.
He says nothing about the drowned kittens.

You cannot fathom him: if you ever find
your own reflection in him, it will be very small.
A long way back, another river joined him; her name was lost in
    his.

He works down at the mill, strong and dependable.
People stop to watch, impressed by his power, his easy grace
with the battling wheel. You are proud of him then.

Now, the dredgers have come.
He sits scared and stiff after the operation.
So grey and quiet in his narrow bed, you hardly dare look.
No swans for weeks.

After Séeberger

La Préfecture, Paris, 19 août 1944 – 'Sans Commentaire'

No good asking her what she thinks –
she's said too much already. Her lips bleed
at the centre of the photograph, where
she's been arranged, surrounded by her betters,
who josh and elbow to get their picture taken,
these dozen lads excused from war today.
One soldier winks. One's just combed his hair.
One's got bad teeth, is grinning anyway.
Someone gestures for the camera with his gun.

She's expressionless. Hard to tell her age.
Dirty dress. She's whitewashed out – could be anyone.
Someone's lent an army tunic, and it's half pulled off
to show her bare neck for the photograph,
the soft round of one shoulder perfectly exposed.

And the men don't wear a proper uniform, except
the GI centre back, with thoughtful cigarette,
who's staring straight at us, not them, direct
from liberated Paris, or anywhere.

Not in this picture: babies, tight-lipped grandmother;
and much earlier, hungry as a lover,
Jean-Claude at his handset, unpacked nightly
from behind loose bricks in her kitchen wall.
She'd lie awake, rehearsing innocence like beads:
barks and footsteps, coded knocking,
urgent German – each sound expected and unbearable.

From beyond the frame an arm is reaching in
to help her raise the heavy caption
whitewashed on a torn-off piece of cardboard box.
They didn't have to hang it round her neck.
Hand angled for the light to catch her wedding ring,
she carries it herself: *She got her husband shot.*

No point asking what, outside the picture,
her plans are for the future, or which lot
it was who shaved off all her hair:
she looks as if the cat has got her tongue.

Pauahi Crater 10 am

I give you this space: the rock at your feet
suddenly gaping. Six hundred paces
of empty air, or air so full of morning
that distance faints. A space full of the years
since its catastrophe, a space of shadow
where, if you fell, you could count seconds down.
Green – perhaps ferns, perhaps ohia trees,
so small, so far away, beyond shouting.

But this pit is full of invisible light
that cannot sing if nothing echoes it.
Nothing can give it shape or scale, until
a white-tailed tropicbird rises into
diagonal volume, trails streamers through
from blossom to star-pink blossom.

ROY BLACKMAN

Roy Blackman was born in 1943 in Burnham, Bucks. He was edu-cated at Bristol University, was awarded a BA with first-class honours from the Open University and received a PhD from the University of Newcastle. For twenty-one years, he worked in 'Marine Pollution Protection' at MAFF.

He won a Hawthornden Fellowship in 1993. His first collection, *As Lords Expected*, was published in 1996, and he has published poems in a wide variety of magazines.

Of the poems in this anthology, 'Even though we don't wear Walkmans' and 'Creating' were first published in the *Oxford Magazine*, 'Not long now' first appeared in *Seam*; an earlier version of 'The Watermen' was published in *Envoi* and 'Turning the kitchen setts' appeared in the *Bridport Prize Anthology* (1996).

Even though we don't wear Walkmans

We stand at the very end of the platform
looking at the rails,

make for the rear of the train and stare
through the window,

sit opposite but far away,
even though we don't wear Walkmans.

Last to rise, the sweep of our gaze
never meets your eyes.

We do not plod, but walk so
slowly, drift with no resilience.

At work we say nothing, or, if
forced to talk, talk only of work;

there's always a reason why
we can't come for a drink.

When we shrink from contact
leave us, help us to survive:

if this were the Third Reich we might be
die Muselmänner. We

are the unsuccessful,
embarrassed to be alive.

Not long now

It's like a brief holiday love-affair:
each seeks reassurance in the other's eyes;
each tries words across this growing silence.
He can still speak, but I must write to him.
Such intimacy can only last another week.

The loved one sleeps. The fan reverses patterns
from the pushed-back bedside light
on one patch of the corner ceiling tiles.
A programmed cabinet blinks silently;
beside me, the night drips steadily by.

He has a man shouting behind his eyes,
takes parts in stimulating morphine plays,
listens hard to death's insistent whispers.
His wide dark pupils stare right through me;
rotting, his mouth exhales the breath of hell.

Soon, life is monosyllabic: 'mouth'; 'drink'; 'hot'.
'Life is hard,' he hesitantly writes
(but death is harder) and then: 'Consider the watch.'
(Paley's? The Morning? With Me? And Pray?).
I do my best, write '3 a.m.', but he is far away.

Back, he pinches the bridge of his nose
in that weary familiar gesture:
how am I to put up with this fool?
The eyes roll up, the big jaw drops:
just how he will look when this breathing stops.

No response for twelve hours overnight,
and then I hear the bubbling begin.
I kiss his cool brow, clasp an unnerving hand,
leave him to the experts, and his next of kin.
Only this February, he was forty.

Turning the kitchen setts

When, having run the blade of a putty-knife
into the cracks between it and its neighbours,
cutting through gunk and oven-crust, fretting
the steadily loosening sand, you finally
ease the first one out and tenderly
brush off its rust and white efflorescence
to see, instead of hollowed crud,
the clean sharp outlines and level surface
in pale oatmeal, or buff of hummus,
unripe dried apricot, fresh avocado flesh,
turmeric, gammon, salmon, paprika,
dark red as deep as unstained beef,
each still glowing, straight from the kiln,
you know why you'll kneel, saw sand for hours,
rasp nails, graze knuckles, numb fingers, raise blisters
to make each local brick give back
what a lifetime's trudge of mud and soot
and grease and grit and dust had lost.

Creating

Is sitting and waiting

getting the sun just right:
not setting, but low daylight
grazing the berm.

Then it's walking steadily, looking
at none of the thousand-and-one
stones you pass at each step
as you sweep that haze, frieze,
fused conglomerate of pebbles
with the inner eye's
focused search-image
of what it is you want to see

till the sun lights on the one stone and you stop,
stoop, pick up the drop, crumb or fleck of fire,
and you have it.

But agate-hunters, I fear, never find amber.

The Watermen

'. . . like watermen, that row one way and look another.'
Robert Burton: The Anatomy of Melancholy

Moving over the moving water,
the water incontinent for sun-sanded sea;
walking beside the running water,
walking under the leaves' cool shade;
climbing to sunshine, leaving the river,
climbing into heather-dust-dry hills to stand
at the bare rock peak of a wind-strewn hill,
silent, alone, to see clearly:
hills, woods, river; the pattern and the path laid out,
and far off, between two now small hills,
the sea;
and know, too small, too far to see:
the brightly-printed metal buckets,
the painted metal and wooden spades.

SASHA DUGDALE

Sasha Dugdale was born in 1974 in Sussex. She read Russian and German at The Queen's College, Oxford and worked as Arts Officer for the British Council in Russia for three years before returning to Britain in 2000. She now works mainly as a writer and translator. She has translated a number of Russian plays for the Royal Court Theatre and BBC Radio Drama, including *Plasticine* by Vassily Sigarev (Nick Hern Books, 2002), *Black Milk* by Vassily Sigarev and *How I Ate a Dog* by Evgeny Grishkovets. Of the poems in this selection, *On Kolomenskoe Embankment* and *Chalk and Cheese* were first published in the *Oxford Magazine; There is Light Streaming* . . . will be published in *The Reader*.

On Kolomenskoe Embankment

All at once a barge came past
Drawing in its skirts the whole river,
And little boys like herrings,
Pale and small with muddy legs,
Clung to the banks, waiting for the wash.

The children of decent families
Sailed past along the embankment
In frothy, ribboned dresses
Arm-in-arm with Mama and
Looking on with longing and disgust.

For Akhmatova

I was a child before I met you.
Small feet in long boat shoes
From my Grandma's cupboard;
And fearlessness:
A fearlessness from not knowing
The world map, my own face
And my soft, soft skin.

We only go forwards, friend.
Life sails down long distance veins,
My milk teeth are strewn about the forest.

Long afternoons staring at a road map:
Europe here, and so this is Yugo
Slavia, and here the trees.

Real tears again and real needs.
Perfume you gave me – I will smell
Like a woman now;
Of fear and longing.

'There is light streaming from an upstairs window'

There is light streaming from an upstairs window
And the door is open.
But you don't notice.
You have your coat on and you are lost in thought.

A bird flies in through the door,
Rises in warm air
Soars from the window
Into the sky and is lost from view.

It could happen a thousand times,
The same quiet circles
The streams of life
The sure deep breathing of the earth.

I was standing there, watching
But you didn't see me.
I placed a hand on your arm
But you didn't feel me.

Now I leave you.
Soon lost from view.
Will you notice?
You have your coat on and you are waiting.

'Under a shower'

Under a shower, in the long
Lighted shed at the works,
After a shift she washes
Her white skin whiter
In a robe of warm water
Falling to her feet

She washes and washes,
Now momentous times have come
A crowd surges and peals
And rushes, holding candles
White and silent and flickering

And boiling around her
Crashing on her arms as she
Lifts them, the torrent bubbles
In her hair – life is changing –

Nothing will be the same
Any more, but she is still
And sculpted in running
Water and sees nothing

But stands there alone
And washes and touches her skin;
Outside armies have marched and wars –
Passed now.

She turns the tap. Shivering, alive,
Dries, dresses in overalls and
Leaves into another world.

Yalta

In Yalta you said you chose friends by the length of their fingers.
The fingers of the Crimea play with the fringe of the sea
My hands are cast down by their sudden rejection
Idling and stubby on the grimy trolleybus seat.
All these Tartar women and the Tsar's high-collared Hausfrau,
All had spindly fingers winding their fates in the lace
Of palaces' long balustrades, over chalky fingers of cliff.

I took your hand in mine and nursed it as if it was you.
You, missing out on the hands of the women I choose,
Theirs, coarsened and blackened, slip apples into our pockets,
Cupped and thicker than glass, they wash our hair at the pump.
And tear the tip from our tickets, and cut the bread at our arm.

And at night on the balcony, the blackened sea below,
Our flat high above Yalta with a map of the land on the wall –
The grasping fingers of Russia, I wound my own in your hair,
And my legs into your body, and silent we both lay there.

Madonna in the Meadow
Giovanni Bellini c.1505

She looks serene but I am sure she is weeping.
She has just been told that the child she holds
Will be dead soon.

The air is thick with the man-made
Consumer of small hearts and lungs.
She was visited at night by a plague cloud;
It sent cinders through the holes burnt in the roof.

A defect, a sad aberration, she was told.
She covers her small garden with sheets
When it rains. She eats little now,
She senses the poison in her gut.

Her husband works in the factory you see behind her.
He knows the danger. They cross themselves
And feel the illness creeping across them.
They eat and touch wood that the food won't enter them.

They are not religious – in fact they have no faith,
These pointless signs are part of a death
They live each day. There is no life here,
Nothing immaculate or God-given.

Letters

I miss our conversations.
I miss the turns around the garden,
The whispered words.

They flew along the pavement,
Barely touching ground
And a lightness filled her.

I pray for strength. I hope for it.
But the nights are full of tears and
Reproaches. My heart is heavy.

Windows of clothes for women
Of another world: sequins, swoops
And the filigree work of costumiers.

I longed for you.
I wrote letters, burned them.
Dreamed of summer, and your return.

Darts, seams and hat feathers
Brushing against them
In their headlong rush.

Now I put pen to paper.
No longer bitter at life.
Facing the reality of my position.

The sky moved as swiftly as they did.
Crossing one street, then another
And out into the open park.

I do not blame you.
You have your own life.
I do not blame you.

Stopping by a bench
They spoke fiercely,
Desire made them angry.

I want to know, though,
You were my friend, I thought.
Were you in love with me?

'I breathed in at night'

I breathed in at night, I'm sure it was you
And in the morning in the creases on my skin
And in my eyes, around my mouth,
You again.

I washed my face of you
Every limb, between my fingers and toes
And my teeth – cleaned of you.

But here you are!
Rubbed on my face, brushed into my hair,
Squeezed on my toothbrush,
Coating my lips, in lines across my eyelids.

Spooned into my mouth. Swallowed.
On the radio and in the clock.
I am sick with you, tired with you,
Yawn you, speak with your voice
And hear it from other mouths.

And then, suddenly, silence. Nothing there
Except a quiet, quiet you inside me.

'The wide glass sky'

The wide glass sky is a perfect circle over the city,
Over yellow houses
Splashed with white
And two soldiers painting a fence
Green with a stick,
Their greatcoats hanging further along.

Rattling along the road, a tram,
Bowling along,
And a woman running behind in a hat,
Black feathers fluttering loose at the brim,

An old street of barrels and baths
And long grey pipes in the sand.
Wind, wind, but no white snow –
Dust and two old men clinking bags
And a woman staring from a window.

This is not mine, this world
These feelings have been stolen
From the unfeeling
These sights have been taken
From the unseeing
This is not mine.

'In a Chinese city'

In a Chinese city the crowds stopped
And the ticking and chirruping of a thousand bicycles
Ceased.
They waited,
One foot on the ground, one poised on the pedal . . .

And all the boats stopped and were blown first this way
Then that by the wind, and always remained in the same map
    square.

An earthquake somewhere: over.
A deathly still covers the villages.
A mute pallbearer leans against a wall and stares.

A train on the sidings stops and the carriages clunk.
The wheels are clasping the rails and singing.
Axles bent like butterfly legs under their load.

A child moans in his sleep and is still. The echo
Of a reedy voice guides the mother in, and she stands,
Silent, wondering whether to touch him.

But it is the moment when the grilles go up,
The birds are singing and a cat-pawed dustbin bag
Shows its entrails open in the street,

That the silence is hard against our touch
Moving back with the night, over the horizon.

Assuming human form

The evening was already there:
The sky split to show a moment's sun,
And something broke inside,
Like thin ice on a puddle.

Emerging, inconspicuous,
From a suburb bound in bindweed
They passed an ancient lake
Of drying dusty mud.

Walking, they kept walking,
The last rays flickered on pebbledash,
The shiny crowns of straggling schoolgirls,
Car roofs, rain stained in the light.

And then darkness crept over.
And there at the end of the road:
A station, two platforms and a mile
Of empty, empty track.

They waited. The board said,
Plan your trip. Last train West . . .
Leave no luggage. And they didn't –
Not so much as a cloven footprint remained.

And I wonder, when the train left,
And they were gone, how many like them
Leaching through the borders, clearings, copses,
Pass through and disappear. We can't know.

Corps de Ballet

In Krasnoyarsk the ballet stars
Ebb and flow together on the stage.
After curtain call and after hours
They strip to music in the theatre bars.

Their bodies are painful to look at,
All snap-fragile and raw ligament,
Close up they are created from greasepaint
Their feet are broken for their art.

They have no abyss of cleavage,
Their ribs lie even as a railway track,
Their hips are narrow as children's,
Their legs as thin and trembling as new calves'.

They perform to wordless, sexless rhythm
On a raised platform by the bar.
Still the drinkers, too desperate for horror,
Hold out cash to go home with them.

And sometimes in the long grass by the theatre
They kneel and open-mouthed accept the blame
For being women in this city, or being
Beyond redemption: it's much the same.

Chalk and Cheese

Grandpa wore a homburg and kid gloves
So small that only I can slip my hands in them.
He ate the same wafers of toast every day
And peaches and cream for pudding.

On a sideboard with a twenty-band wireless inside,
(Monaco, Luxembourg, Berlin, Stockholm)
He kept a silver retirement plate from the Directors
And portrait photographs of my Aunt and Mum.

Sprawling on the deck in a gown,
Leaning from a cruiser in a Hamburg harbour.
He met a host of swastikas with polite hostility.
A small man, preoccupied. As far from me as chalk.

Grandma wrote to me for a long time. I didn't treasure
As I should have done, her strange life, the patchwork
On the sofa, the field at the end of the garden. She went to
Switzerland and Germany, when the moon was closer.

Her friends had Ho Chi Minh and Mao on their walls
She sent parcels to the East, complained once that
Peter Rabbit was censored, even though he filched
The lettuce from the fat man. As far from me as cheese.

And what of us? Will we fill a form for our childrens'
Children? Will they sum us up in verses or will they say,
As we feel ourselves to be, they were all chalk and cheese.
They were all contradiction and fear. They made no sense.

STUART HENSON

Stuart Henson was born in Huntingdonshire in 1954. After studying in Nottingham and Lock Haven, USA, he returned to Huntingdon, where he still lives and works. He received an Eric Gregory Award in 1979 and has published two collections, *The Impossible Jigsaw* (1985) and *Ember Music* (1994) with Peterloo Poets. A booklet of poems to accompany drawings by artist Mark Bennett, *Clair de Lune*, was published by Shoestring Press in 1998 and a full-length narrative sequence, *A Place Apart*, set in England and Canada, is due from Shoestring in 2003. His writing for children includes play adaptations of Ian Serraillier's *The Silver Sword*, John Steinbeck's *The Pearl*, and the picture-book *Who Can Tell?* with illustrations by Wayne Anderson.

Of the poems in this anthology, 'The Cannonball' first appeared in *Poetry Wales* and 'Up There' was first published in *The Hudson Review*. The Cemetery of the Four Knolls, in the second part of 'Mountain Time', lies about a mile outside the gold-rush settlement of Tin Cup, Colorado.

The Train to Nowhere

The wheels are welded to the track
by volts of frost:
degrees too deep to be imagined.
Stasis, vast as a continent.
A godless horizon.
There are only causes.
The blood shrinks from fingers and feet
as mercury retreats
to the bleb of a thermometer.
Man is the measure.
And the torturer takes a precise interest
in the calibration of what can be borne.
He is inclined to poeticise
his investigations:
the Swallow, the Wishbone, the Elephant . . .
There is no going back.
(There is no locomotive)
Only the wind, seething under the carriages.
A woman is coughing
like an engine failing to start.
And round that a raging silence
from all the guns
of Cechnya and Ingushetia.

The Cannonball

The scar was on the ditch side
and hidden like conspiracy.
I was five maybe
when my granddad showed me
the roundel, the ringworm
in the bark where he
and his mates had plugged
a great steel shot
as big as a cricketball
in the bole of the tree.

And you could feel the place
and see the green wound
healing into history.
A cannon ball.
I checked it secretly
and told no one.
And I believed in iron
closed in the heartwood's depth,
the knots, the dark shakes,
growing, becoming a part of me.

Under the Shadows

Under the shadows of the great trees
I watch you go, with your light stride,
oblivious that I am watching and must know
how I shall lose to shadows and their kind
all love's dumb familiars in due time.

The dark sequoias draw you down
their long perspective like the last frames
of a film that leaves its plot untied.
Only the spaces grow and grow,
and the ache of something wide and undefined.

The trees have simple thoughts and simple lives.
Their limbs are scooped as if to reach
and hide you, and I can't decide
if they are sinister or seek to shelter
you with spirits I might call benign.

There is no music now, no sound.
If I should shout, it would be drowned
in silence and the avenue of dark trees
where you step on unheeding, out of sight,
beyond the shadow-fields, dissolved in light.

from *Mountain Time*

1

UP THERE

at ten thousand feet
you run for half a football pitch's length
and, breathless, you realise the body's just
a machine for living in.
You're nearer, there, to the spinning firmament
and the air's pure
but mean with its oxygen.

At night you lie down
and the bone of the mountain's uncomfortably
close to your own, the sky's membrane
is pricked through with stars,
and the roof of your tent
where the seeds fall, steadily, like rain,
is uncomfortably thin.

When you wake
and the moon has risen above the peaks,
in a moment of disbelief you believe
that you're lying in snow,
that you froze; the machine stopped; that
your soul is about to take
a step into heaven – or oblivion.

2

CEMETERY OF THE FOUR KNOLLS

Protestant Knoll:

So death is a wood
a pathless way
We cannot skirt it round
or stay

or we lose ourselves
in trees and shades
where the sunlights play

Jewish Knoll:

Now we are separate
always
even in death

And even here
at the end of the Earth

At night the skies
are cold and clear

The stars are scattered over our graves
like a lost people

Catholic Knoll:

The flames
burning in their little cups

so white and small
they are almost invisible

and dipping
white in the sunlight

so pale they are blown
to nothing by the slightest breeze

O Mary, Virgin, Mother of God
be with us here
among the shawled peaks

your colour our colour
wrapping the skies

Boot Hill:

We knew how to live –
in the canyon
and in the whore-house

We knew how to duck
before we saw
the smoking forty-five

Rock-fall   Treachery   Sclerosis   Syphilis
We gambled high

and we laughed at the grocers
the storekeepers then
with their nagging wives

The wind sighs here like pleasure
and the gap-toothed peaks
that we measured ourselves against
still ring us round

In the summer the earth
is dry and warm under needle-fall

We never claimed to be God-fearing men

There are worse places to be
than under the ground

MARTHA KAPOS

Martha Kapos was born in Connecticut in 1941 and grew up in Cambridge, Massachusetts. She completed a degree in Classics at Harvard, then came to London to study Painting and the History of Art at the Chelsea School of Art, where she stayed to teach, lecturing and writing on art and poetry until 2001. Her first poetry publication was a pamphlet, *The Boy Under the Water*, from the Many Press in 1989. She won a Hawthornden Fellowship in 1994 and in 2000 was shortlisted for *Poetry Review*'s Geoffrey Dearmer 'Poet of the Year' award. In 2001 she became assistant poetry editor of *Poetry London*. *My Nights in Cupid's Palace*, coming out from Enitharmon in 2003, will be her first collection.

Of the poems in this anthology 'The Night Kitchen' and 'Pantomime' were first published in *Poetry Review*, 'An Angel Entered the Picture' and 'Tree-Poem for Apollo' in *Poetry London*, 'Mute' in the *Times Literary Supplement*, 'Yes and No' in *Other Poetry*, and 'The Origin of the Sexes According to Aristophanes' in *Staple*.

The Night Kitchen

Outside extinct stars hang
like scrunched-up letters thrown
around the floor. The earth is poised
on a hook above the sink.
An enormous sponge sits planetary and alone
in its enamel dish. So if I notice

a cracked glass face-down needs chucking out,
the draining-board is chipped by something
dropped last year, the forks all look
faintly yellow between their prongs,
why do my arms wrapped in mist in the fairy liquid
feel the long warm pull of the tide,

why is it suddenly all
a darkness of islands in oceans, the inconstant soap
a slab of light slipping between my fingers
like a moon? And if the folded
dishcloth rises to a pinnacle of hope
against an embroidery of midnight-blue,

and if the bubbles coming on and going out
range themselves in a white ring big
as the Crab Nebula, and if I'm floating
inches above the ground, the pocket in my apron
growing into a pouch so large that it could hold
Medusa's head, J-cloths flapping

from my heels like the wings of Mercury,
and through the hazy half-dark I begin to see
a constellation in a drift of dust,
puddles on the floor big enough to hold the Milky Way,
will you keep the earth's poles

together between your firm hands, administer
the law of gravity, and hold onto all
the rattling atoms of the world?

An Angel Entered the Picture

Years of careful work had made
the illusion perfect.

A stroke of grey was like the sky
divided from brown by a long neat line

we believed was the horizon.
Up and down were like the fixed stars.

Rocks lay still. In angled shadows
houses looked exactly sharpened.

Trees stood rooted to the spot
as if the law of gravity

had been a religion, then stepped back
in graduated sizes to the smaller

thinner blue as we knew they would.
The picture resembled life so closely

mist rose straight up from the lawn.
Then an angel entered.

Red went right through to the centre
where there were two hearts.

Beating together, main arteries linked
in intense traffic, the red

filling with red and rising
even to the words on our lips.

Remember how we saw
the frame peel away, the air glisten

like daylight without its skin.
And how, leaping out of bed,

we threw the window open to find
a breeze was blowing.

Yes and No

Even before you were born you
lived in her intricate hands.

She would leave them open
like messages on the table

saying yes and saying no,
two unfolded maps of a country

where the sea behaved like theft
and disappeared or loomed

round and white, sent
sheets of rapid milk

across the sand, but only
for a moment, then tugged them back,

smoothing and smoothing a new place
fresh as humiliation.

Even before you were born you
lived in her absent-minded

smile. A surprise appearance
of the sun had nothing

on the way it spilled
into a sudden arc stretched out

to hold you. Or let you go.
Smiling her smile. And there it was:

the open secret she wore inside out
showing its label by mistake.

Even before you were born you
lived in her chambered heart.

Two up, two down when you
were wrapped up small

as a glimpse, the double doors
swung you both ways, beat

you in their pulse, carried
you abruptly on the tide

of their in and out, cradled you,
and whispered cold in the warm air.

Mute

Tree as empty as a house
when your mother is not at home,
few or yellow or promising
they will come back, your syllables
are loose circles blown about
barely forming words, your leaves
amount to nothing without her saying
You look lovely standing there
in your hair and your dress.

Equator

When she held your small heart tight as the equator,
she was immense. Houses bobbed up and down
around her as she turned in the bed of the world,
her body lifting and falling like the sea.

With one sweep of her hand, towns were wiped
from the face of the earth. She left the wrinkled
shore fine as a sheet. In propitious weather
her breath had the regularity of day.

It was then a touch of her finger was an earthquake
filmed in reverse. Towns reappeared. Bricks rose
into place, jumping from the sinking dust.
Lost days scattered on the floor were threaded

back like history on a knotted string. When her
arms once ringed the sky and drew
the circumference of everything in sight,
you stood like a little tower on her lap
balanced by the tip of her finger.

Cosmology

When her face gazing down
at one time held a sun
people would tell each other stories

about how the earth spoke
in green details after a long silence,
about how the trees would come out

of doors to celebrate and stand around
in voluble groups outdoing themselves
stirring, fleshing, flowering.

People would get down on their knees
as it passed across the sky like a woman
moving from room to room in a house.

She sits down to comb her hair and she is
the incandescent centre in the envelope,
the blue long-awaited letter torn open

to let us see its one shining point
of reference, and there in a cloudy system of worlds

the weather is clear.
It's late afternoon in early spring.
The light is falling on a certain tree.

A Child is the Sea

But it's that letting go I want.
The sea was banging its crib.
It was rocking back and forth
in the small turmoil
of a child in a dark room alone.

The sun had blown out for good
taking with it every light.
With no intention of coming back
without an apology. *But what is my body for
if it's not for you?* The sea sulked.

It crouched and rippled
then lay sly as a plate watching
the sky, scanning its empty grey-blue walls
for a door that might open for you
to come in as if nothing had happened.

Intent on her face the sea sat
in the lap of the sky. *You fill*
the world when you're this close.
The sea talked, but only by watching
the other's mouth: a flickering blue

full of devices of light
it stole from the sky and pretended to own.
Slowly working at closing, opening, closing,
the waves mouthed themselves
to make the words come alive.

But each dumb shape just lolled
without insisting,
like a dead tongue on a slab,
with no real form of its own,
or stuttered at a whim of the wind.

So the sea led them in to the beach
dreaming of the tenderness of milk,
then slammed and slammed,
each meek wave lifted, tucked under
and crushed on the stones.

It's that letting go I want.
To be loved and destroyed, loved
and destroyed. That letting go in which
I am washed away. But all she wanted
was to stand on the beach as if

it was solid rock. The sun
would enter the sea's blue-black dream,
lunging and shimmering,
and be right there in the moments after sleep,
coming, going and coming back all

on the same day. She wanted one word
held back to wait in a cry,
to be the tear that had to be wept
first, that would then fall
gigantic and multiple as rain.

She wanted to hear its placatory
consoling sounds, when joking together
they would both come, in a little while,
to tuck her in, the light between them
growing them together in a broad smile.

She wanted to fasten
their words together, to weave herself
into their voluble talk,
you moving, I moving inside you,
to be lost in the seamless whisper:

the sound through the window of the waves
never completely breaking.

The Narrow Kiss

The wooded path takes an unfamiliar
swing to the left. Immediately
the sky is open for business.
The flat sea is wrinkling

its face, throws back its head in a laugh.
As if we had been children together
the blue water runs with me.
The horizon keeps up from a distance

like a song I don't know by heart.
An aching line reaches all the way
to remind me: this is where we went
taking a map that was only a wish.

It is where we were always together.
Come again into the open
inside of the fruit, into the white
inexhaustible milk. Come again into

the quick. It is where overnight,
following the gentlest law, the skin
also opened, where we were not surface
any longer but voluminous and sea-deep.

Where two mouths formed a narrow
kiss we slipped through, we swam
in the green room of ourselves breathing
the impossible breath of fish.

But now the sun is high and blurred.
Trees pass preoccupied and turn away
wrapped up inside their leaves.
The sea has stepped back into

a blue glimpse behind the trees – but you,
the water I see : your laughing voice,
your gestures touching the sand
still remind me of someone I know.

Pantomime

Faces facing across the table,
this is when we lift the lid
off the box, take out the flat
brown suit, then gravely as a crown

loop the tunnel of the neck
over our heads, unroll the four
rumpled legs, step in and run the zip
up the stomach. This is better

than we thought: the bronze rump
shining in the sun, the velvet lips,
the curve of the intelligent neck.
Sit back and watch the perfect

half-wit smile spread. Swaying
gently like a milk-float
(to light applause) tiny
goose-steps locked

we tinker up onto the stage.
I spill a long wet tongue
from the mouth. You aim a graceful
squirt of milk from the penis

(a standing ovation) push
a spot-lit hand through to wag the tail.
Sausages are gliding in a pink heap
onto the floor. We paw the earth,

lower the dynamic head and take
several fences. Now we're floating
high over the steep hills and far away.
Yes it is. No it's not – a large

crumpled heap of corduroy on the floor.
Don't miss it. Our double act
zipped up together in the semi-dark,
heads I win, tails you lose,

is for this limited season only.
We collapse the legs, rub out
the eyes, take up the ears by the roots.
But hold on. The stable-door is locked.

This bolting horse is a cuckoo
in the nest, a marching army of occupation,
an enormous tongue in the mouth.
It will run and run.

Tree-Poem for Apollo

My fingertips are planning their escape.
There go my hands up over my head,
they ease out ten long buds,

each one sticking out its tongue:
a wet green stalk
and a leaf. I am speaking to you now

only through the vocabulary of leaves:
how they are open and continually open,
the rush of sap

where the stem begins
the too-much-detail of their veins,
the daft shine on their faces

as they fall all over themselves
to see the sun,
the way they have of blurting out *green! green!*

All these things I say out loud,
but, for you, I disappear into an instant
tunnel of bark, furred-over, hidden.

How can my body go
into such abeyance that I become
only a thin blonde ring of growth,

so far down in the centre of the trunk,
I'm lost as the small private O
shining at the bottom of a well.

Deep as an animal brain
ticking its secret

on unknown frequencies inside
the smooth stroked head
under your hand.

The Origin of the Sexes
According to Aristophanes

Our simplicity of feeling was an explosion.
Fireworks – especially Catherine wheels
circled the sky. We spun out
head-over-heels an elated shower
of lights. We had at least two heads,
four arms and legs, and several tongues.
Spikes grew from the fingers of our
unclenched hands; a thousand forms burst
with a deafening report from our beating
hearts. Our high voices rolled
the length of the horizon for hours on end
without falling. We were blue touch-paper,
rings of hung mist, red-haloed chisel-points
in the dark. Shooting stars had nothing on our
full speed, forced landings in mid-air,
our perfect incendiary curves.
Our ascent to heaven would surely
take place at any moment; and the rest
of the world backed away, for who
can embrace a fire? 'This perfection must stop!'
A god stepped in. The swift parting slice
of an axe. Since then the lights have dimmed,
and we must hobble on the earth on two legs.

The Blackberry

Your face is a cipher when your smile
splays out into the many

double directions a child takes on a walk,
twirling a stem of grass in an erratic

circle of two minds
Do I want this? Do I want this?

The smile on its way to your face
dawdles, lost in thought.

It is stopping to pick blackberries
on the hot path. The dangling

things on the verge of having
must hold still under the leaves.

Lift the berry slowly
between your thumb and forefinger

so it slips off whole from the stem,
all of its loose possibilities

you softly swallow, intact in your mouth,
the round knob of syllables

making one word that sounds exactly right.
But its double kiss, thicketed and warm,

is a little white lie
cuffed in fur. Hard losing itself

in soft, fusty and sweet, like hearing
your own voice all wrong.

Smash it like the toy you didn't want
against a wall. If you could only

hold everything dark-coloured on your tongue
forever without breaking:

little reds becoming black
scripts written on your lips.

HUGH McMILLAN

Hugh McMillan was born in 1955, and was educated at Dumfries Academy and Edinburgh University. He currently teaches history in Dumfries. He has had three books of poetry published: *Tramontana* (1990, Dog and Bone); *Harridge* (1994, Chapman); and *Aphrodite's Anorak* (1996, Peterloo).

Some of the poems in this anthology have appeared previously in the *Herald, Cencrastus, Northwords* and *New Writing Scotland*. 'A Very Short History of the Darien Scheme' appeared as a poster in the Royal Museum of Scotland's exhibition on the Scottish Diaspora.

Wandered

He is visiting his old mother.
Sunlight is fading, leaves crunch under his boots.
When he arrives she is standing by the window,
tapping her small foot.
'Where have you been this last twenty years?'
she asks, anger in her dark and skittish eyes.

It is an old scenario.
The truth will only breed confusion,
worse, a dreadful sadness.
'I have been in orbit,' he replies,
'It is the longest manned flight in space
by any Scotsman.'

She squeezes his arm,
her face soft as a girl's.
'I am proud of you Willie,' she says,
'I never doubted you would return',
and they sit and watch
as the stars come out over Gorgie.

My Mother's Dictionary

The pages curl back from *arcane*
all the way to *chabazite*
and a paper black with anagrams,
epsils, sepisle, sleep is, sleep is.
Some words are marked.
Otherness in bold red pen, *tutelage.*
Near *Spring*
there's a parchment of a leaf.
In the margin by *violin*,
the name *O'Brien*,
mysteriously underlined.

Fanning the pages is to breathe her in,
to the point you can imagine, *witchcraft*,
her back by that roaring fire, smoke curling,
and words circling her legs like cats.

A Curse on Sister Owens

Picture the scene:
a field hospital in Tripoli,
my father close to pulp.
A nurse, I imagine her

slim, high boned,
an English rose,
is sending back
my mother's note.

'In his present state,'
she writes (unruffled by the heat,
I bet, a Prefect of the charnel house)
'I fear this dreadful news

would be too much.'
So I have this pious bitch
to thank then

for these winter streets,
and all the afternoons
chasing my reflection
through the puddles of Dumfries.

I have her to praise
for the Sunday League abuse,
the coverings-up and making do,
Ayrshire gulag holidays

and bug-eyed Aunts,
hidden treasuries of guilt,
and the sense that anything
half good can't last,

for the apocalypse of genes
that Sister Owens arranged,
all my disasters in waiting.

Sometimes I dream of my Free French father,
last spotted, they think, in a photo,
sleeping by his Spitfire.
Behind him slow clouds unroll

over hop fields.
He got through the Summer's
dangers unscathed,
with his scarf and Labrador.

I have seen him since, in magazines
and café society.
He is a philosopher, or novelist.
He has lovers and wives.

He is golden. The sun is everywhere:
on his face, his hair,
the place not taken.

Old Photograph

It is VE night, Tobermory.
Cottages blaze and shimmer in the mirror of the bay.
Light is necklaced everywhere,
on the cross-trees of destroyers,
on the hulls of every cockleshell and scalloper afloat,
even on the gutted snout of a U-boat,

but there are shadows, to imagine
the black and frozen water
and the land, lonely of men,
from Sunart to Mers el Kébir.

Daisy chained by sailors, three WAAFs
pose for a photograph.
Her friends are grinning, wide-eyed,
but my mother's smile is dying
and she's turned away
to the sound of the waves,
as if she could sense my father,
whose war would never cease,
limping inexorably back to her
across the oil scarred sea.

Wildlife

To the Director, Highland Regional Council.
Dear Sir,
Last Friday I left my hotel early
to catch the bus from Lochinver,
the better to observe the fauna
and grandeur of your Highland scenery.
I was not at first distressed
to find that this vehicle was the school bus,
for the people of the north west,
(my adjutant was from Bunessan),
are of noble stock.
I was depressed, however, that
my reveries on Munros and stacs
were interrupted by a loud blast
of music from someone called Fatboy Slim.
Later, when I spoke to the driver, remarked to him
about the way the stags were tossing
their heads,
there was an outbreak of sniggering

behind me. Then, when I thought I'd spotted
a sea eagle, I was hit in the ear
by a packet of cheese and onion crisps
followed sharply by a crushed drinks container.
Of course I turned round at this,
whereupon a strumpet with nose jewellery
such as Hindu women have
said, albeit in lilting and lyrical way,
'What are you looking at, you baldy bastard?'
I understand there are many tinker children
in the west,
but I feel compelled to draw to your attention
the fact that these incidents
spoiled for myself and my wife
what in other circumstances might
have been an educational insight
into Highland life.

Marked

Linn McGarr,
I am marking your exam in the bar,
a highly unethical thing to do.
It's quite true,
as my own experience confirms,
that ten pints may harm
the critical facility,
my famed integrity.

I have no choice, Linn McGarr.
I have taken on a thousand papers
so that myself and Jane
can go on our honeymoon to Spain.
I have to mark them constantly,
on the bus, at the toilet, in my sleep.
It is a hard and desperate life, McG,
I suspect you would concur with me.

And the pub is not so bad.
Summer stabs
through little slats of window,
corkscrews of dust glow,
dance in their spotlights,
rich gantry green and ambers ignite.
Are you in the sun, Linn McGarr?
Is it sparking concretes in Craigmillar?

I see, Linn McGarr,
you think Asquith was murdered
by Emily Pankhurst in 1903.
After another pint I am tempted to agree
(his later photographs show a corpse-like pallor)
and Trotsky, you say, overthrew Stalin.
Credit will always be given
to valid pieces of wishful thinking,

and your response to the Triple Entente,
'Who cares?' seems sublime, succinct,
though it's not in the marking scheme,
and I like the way you dot the 'i' in Linn,
like a little bubble hovering in space,
above the mediocrity of name and place.

It is strange how fate has done us in.
If I had my way, Linn,
people like you and I would stride out
on the by-ways of history like giants.
Life has other plans for you, me too perhaps.
In the meantime, for what it's worth, full marks.

A Very Short History of the Darien Scheme

We turned up in the tropics to try our luck,
the Indians told us to get to fuck,
but we were very soon the best of pals
over bottles of whisky and hot mescal.
Then next we're on the forest floor,
trying to wrestle conquistadors,
in plate armour to add insult,
but we beat them. What a result!
Then no bastard turns up with fresh supplies,
so we died,
or spawned generations of freckled Hottentots:
England at fault.

Room 3

Somewhere outside,
children are singing,
gutters groan with starlings,
doors slam, gears jam,
butter melts on acrid toast,
but in Room Three,
the curtains closed,
the light champagne green,
I trace rare histories
in rumpled sheets,
in wisps of scent,
in echoes of pandemonium.

This place,
tilting on the edge of probabilities,
with its scone mountains,
its *fin-de-siècle* chambermaids,
is somehow privy
to a pure and fierce reality.
I recline,

watch the clouds
and the far off swim of sandstone,
and spend the day
looking for what's lost,
your rings, your watch,
me.

On the Coast of North West England

Willowherbs through ribs of iron fret
and red flowers of rust.
Grey houses scattered by the wind

plant and bud
blunt kids, skimming stones on sad beaches
thinking of America,

and the arcades at the end of the world.
Dregg, Flimby, Netherton,
in the armpits of dead factories,

their curtains closed
as the sea lies limp at their doors,
the fog just off shore vague like old nightmares.

In Maryport men from the pubs
lug back chips
as the gulls, mimicking their fathers,

follow the little wake home.

The Curse of Atreus

Cicadas saw the air
and tired blooms nod their last today.
On stilts of polished stone Mycenae swims,
its memories sour as old uranium,
that deadly clock still turning round.
But this afternoon others are as loud.
Andrew and Teri sit,
their blonde hair mixed
in a burn of gold.
I am not staring at the face of Agamemnon
but Tithonus.
They pass the day dreaming of a single kiss
while I watch the river beds gouged like half healed cuts
and the buses grunt away like beasts,
and feel each second torn away
from me like nails.

Remember

Remember me in barlight,
flanked by limping men,
on football fields at twilight, shooting long balls in,
near green lacquered mountains
with cold water by,
on a staircase playing robots
with a tireless little boy.
May large chested women mourn me,
and forgive me all my turns,
my love was shrapnelled like the sun,
but like shrapnel always burned.
I'd like taxi drivers and poets
to tell lies and sing,
I'd like tears and pies and fisticuffs,
in fact almost anything,

and at 2 am
I'd like you to look out at the moon,
and drink and snog, make promises,
imagine you'll see me soon.

RICHARD MEIER

Richard Meier was born in Epsom in 1970, was educated in Surrey and Manchester, and now lives and works in London.

'Solo' and 'Relative' have been published before in *The North*; 'Ablutions', 'Dreamlike' and 'Tracing Paper' first appeared in *PN Review*.

Dreamlike

And I was afloat, onboard what I took
to be an ark, an ark which housed a world,
a perfect one I felt, where everything
had at long last secured its long-lost half:
apple pips paired with baby squirrels' eyes,
rained-on puddles with rings in a jewellery box,
contour lines showing gentle hills with birch grain,
space with time, and so on; and you of course,
you were there, yet you refused to sit with me,
choosing instead the company of doves
(paired unconvincingly I thought, at first,
with snow); sending one out, you expressed hope
it might come back with something in its beak –
at which point my mind cleared. And that was that.

Phil

You probably know someone like Phil: the type
of guy who one day into his latest job
speaks of *we*, meaning his new company;
who sports the sort of gear everyone's wearing,
yet considers himself to be discerning;
is neutral when it comes to nature – 'flowers
and that' – in fact, whole seasons can pass him by;
but is open to new things:
got into sushi briefly and, before that, karting.

At times, you can almost touch someone real
beneath the spiel; that's when you warm to him
or gather, rather, someone's there to warm *to*:
the evening, for example, he let on
how he's a mystery to his family –
the suits, the job – Phil's someone who, just when
you're congratulating yourself on being genuine,
brings you up short: to him, clearly,
he's his own creation, just as much as you are.

Always chipper, he's the kind of bloke
who'll strike people as being *genuinely* happy –
much more so than you might – and yet, for all that,
what you feel for him is sympathy.
Or is that what you nearly feel? There must
be times, no, when the front just falls away,
moments of impossible clarity
when he's plain Phil? There must be times,
surely. At least you'd wish them on him, wouldn't you.

Ablutions
for Imogen

That's strange, I'll think, some afternoons
and make to turn off the bathroom light
I'm all but sure I've not left on . . .

only to catch, for the umpteenth time,
the frosted windows splintering sunlight
like it's hitting water, and stand –

as one who needs reminding – stunned
how sometimes there's just so much light,
and how it is I never learn.

Adults

When they'd ask me *So, how's school?* or
How's the piano coming along? and
maybe deem my mumbling 'shyness',
I'd want to ask them – quid pro quo –
So, how's your marriage? How's your job?,
but couldn't knowing I was the child,
yet also since at times I'd sense in them
some great weight of grown-up sadness
warning how they might just tell me
and it would all be much too much
for them to handle, me to hold.

Solo

Back in St Lucia, where Januaries
can top ninety, his name *Janvier* carries
none of the coldness it can take on here
and which matches his mien, like winter sun
all the warmth's been creamed off from.

At the jobclub he hands me a form –
some health and safety training caper
for the demolition work he's always done,
until, that is, these lightless weeks
of warehouse dawns and forklift shifts
to forestall this, his signing on.

School? I ask him, halfway through the form –
We never had no school in St Lucia
he chuckles right through me, slapping
the butcher's block of his thigh, his voice
soft as his *Don't you 'brother' me* one-liner
that silenced a guy earlier who'd been too pally.

I saw him once, climbing down from his crane,
its fuck-off conker swaying to a plumbline.
Behind it, for one night, a two-up two-down
had realised its dream to become the end-of-terrace –
its parlous bedrooms, its bombsite lounge
open to the evening, and raw as that feeling,
the worst, that you owed someone.

In Case of Fire
for Lisa

And whereas I had said *Letters and photos*,
and seen myself muscling through the flames,

you would go back especially for your houseplants –
these dreamy weeping figs, this stocky yucca –

what's worth remembering remembered, leaving
both hands free for carrying out the future.

Tracing Paper

The weather felt familiar:
the mist's matt white stemming the view
across the moor; the intrinsic
raininess. And likewise the stone,
that rough-faced, scorched-looking gritstone
Ilkley's built from. Four when I left,

the year my father's firm posted
us all down south, it's these rocks though,
the Cow and Calf, perched on the hill –
the squat ex-quarry Cow watching
over the smaller, yet house-sized, Calf –
which have stayed with me the most.
As I climbed towards them, I found

myself trying to recreate
the memory, the still, I've always
carried; how strange I must have looked,
adjusting my positioning
(the two rocks now huge cut-out shapes
découpaged/pasted to the sky),
sliding this view over the first one,
determined to have the two fit.

Relative

In the Sixties, of course, no one ever
said no, he starts for my benefit.
Like witnesses, his mates chip in,
backing him up, flush with examples,
staggered still how easy it was then.
Fresh out of college, I sit there nodding,
mock agog at my glum uncle
and cocky enough, then, to dismiss
what he deems the closest to paradise
you could ever come. *Just imagine,*
he marvels – *everywhere you walked,*
everywhere you looked, work, work, work.